THE HESS TOY COLLECTOR

PLATINUM EDITION

The content of this book represents an accumulation of information that the author has derived through many years of collecting. Also, hours of interviews were conducted to assure the story presents factual data. However, due to the nature of the subject, no claim can be made as to its absolute correctness. F.S.B.O., or anyone associated with F.S.B.O., cannot be held responsible for any errors or omissions made within this book. The book merely represents information that is correct to the best of our knowledge and in no way is associated with, nor authorized by, the Amerada Hess Corporation of Woodbridge, NJ.

THE HESS TOY COLLECTOR

PLATINUM EDITION

Author - Michael V. Harwood
Photographer - William E. Taylor III
Editor - Gaye Gravely Pollitt

F.S.B.O. Books - Englewood, NJ

F.S.B.O. Books
are published by
F.S.B.O. Inc.
117 Cedar Lane
Englewood, NJ 07631

Platinum Edition - 1 of 5000

Library of Congress Card Number: 96-85153
ISBN 0-9630345-2-9

Printed by: H&K Litho, Inc. Clifton, New Jersey
Printed in USA.

THE HESS TOY COLLECTOR

PLATINUM EDITION

1170

of 5000

michael Harwood

For my family,

Eva, Judi and Michael

To the reader

Much of the material in this book comes from my own observations over a period of 31 years, beginning in the winter of 1964, and from many interviews with collectors, colleagues and particularly with those persons directly involved.

Since my last writing of this book some five years ago, additional information has surfaced and I have learned many new things. Although my first book was accurate and received recognition and "congratulations for a very professional accomplishment" from Mr. Leon Hess, Chairman of the Board, I feel we now have an even more accurate account of the history of this magnificent collectible given to us annually by Amerada Hess Corporation of Woodbridge, New Jersey.

Michael V. Harwood

June 1996

Contents

Preface

The history begins in 1964 when a company, then called the Hess Oil and Chemical Corporation, home office Perth Amboy, New Jersey, started selling a limited edition plastic toy vehicle. Each year since then (with few exceptions) right around Thanksgiving Day, Hess has offered their customers a fine quality, delicately detailed replica of a Hess Oil Company vehicle. Only offered at Hess service stations along the East Coast, these beautifully designed vehicles are sold until supplies run out, invariably before the holiday buying season ends.

Suspense and excitement build months before the holidays with speculation and rumors flying about the next toy design. Many customers, collectors and children patiently — and sometimes not so patiently — wait to see what the new model year will bring. The Hess people themselves stay as tight-lipped as possible about the secret design to surprise everyone on opening sales day.

Each year a growing number of people, from young children to the most avid toy collectors, anxiously wait to add the new vehicle to their collection. As a teenager growing up in New Jersey, I could hardly wait to see what the creative people at Hess would produce. To this day, I find myself listening to the rumors and cruising by Hess service stations to catch a glimpse of the models before they are marketed.

People ask why all the excitement over a plastic toy? And why has this become one of the hottest and most desirable collectibles of the 90's? The answers are **quality** and **value.**

First, let's talk about **quality**. The vehicle itself is designed and made exclusively for Hess Oil Company, unlike promotional items sold by many other oil companies who simply put their paint schemes and logos on current production, off-the-shelf toys. Hess never even considered doing this.

From design drawing board to the Hess customer, utmost care is given to each detail. Stringent manufacturing procedures go into every toy with constant quality control and supervision throughout the entire process. Since the majority of their "customers" are children, Hess devotes special care to assure all safety standards regarding design and use are met. They've also gone the extra step of prominently displaying a special message on certain toys. The boxes state, " Caution! Due to small parts, not recommended for children under three years old." And since1988, Hess has extended its warning to include children under four.

The multi-colored box is as sturdy as the toy inside. Displaying silk-screened pictures of various Hess facilities and warm holiday scenes, the box is beautiful. This well packed box includes instructions such as how to install batteries, and how to operate working head and tail lights. For a few of the more recent models, directions explain how to operate the newly added switches that activate realistic sounding sirens, horns, and in 1995, even the rotating blades on their Helicopter. Alkaline batteries are always included for each toy — in itself a unique feature.

Many oil companies have since picked up on Mr. Hess' creative marketing concept, but none have equaled his quality. The greatest compliment to the toys' quality would be to say that many serious collectors and modelers feel like I do that these promotional vehicles from Hess are "a work of art."

Now let's look at **value**. I personally feel Hess Oil Company has given the buyer unequaled value - from the price in 1964 of a $1.39 including batteries to the 1995 price of $15.99. No other toy sold as a promotional item can compare. Nor does Hess require a gas or oil purchase at the service stations to obtain a toy. It's safe to assume that, at best, the Company can only be breaking even on this promotion. This is their way of saying "thank you" to their loyal customers and "happy holidays" to children everywhere. It has become a tradition in many families on the East Coast to have a Hess truck under the Christmas tree every year.

In the last few years, Hess introduced purchase restrictions, limiting the buyer to two toys. With these restrictions, toys remain in inventory at the service stations longer, giving the Hess customer enough time to purchase them. Simultaneously, it keeps

Line at Hess Station Was for Toy Cars

By MICHAEL POLLAK

An oil company is caught short by the demand for a holiday promotion.

The Christmas shopping season is just about over at Amerada Hess's 535 gas stations on the East Coast. After two weeks of sellouts and short tempers, the company still has plenty of gasoline, but a shortage of toy police cars.

The surge in demand for the toys caught the company — which has been selling different models each year starting on Thanksgiving Day for 30 years — by surprise. In New York and New Jersey, there were long lines even while the turkeys were cooling, as regular station customers and families hoping to fill stockings competed with a growing number of toy collectors.

Hess ordered about 1.5 million of this year's model, a police patrol car with flashing lights and siren, about 15 percent more than last year, said Carl T. Tursi, vice president and corporate secretary of the Amerada Hess Corporation.

The company, which is based in New York, stopped running its advertisements on Dec. 3, realizing that it would run out of the toys well before Christmas. Yesterday, a message on the company's toy information telephone number, (800) 748-9763, said only four stations were still being supplied. The four are at 10th Avenue and 45th Street in Manhattan; Route 9 South in Woodbridge, N.J.; Route 22 and Memorial Parkway in Phillipsburg, N.J., and Islip Avenue in Central Islip, L.I.

Reasons for the run are not hard to find. Since 1964, when Leon Hess suggested selling a model of his company's tank truck to call attention to his stations, Hess trucks have been sold at low prices. This year's price is $11.99, which includes two new batteries. Made by the Louis Marx toy company until 1971 and now made in China, the vehicles have a reputation for durability and style and have become a tradition for a generation of children. Many of the recipients are now adults with money to spend.

For example, the 1964 model, which cost $1.29 when new, can sell for $2,500 in mint condition through toy fairs and collector magazines.

"We don't cooperate with collectors," Mr. Tursi said. Hess station managers are told to limit sales to two to a customer. Deliveries are sporadic and spread out.

Next Year Will Be Different

Hess, which does not require truck buyers to buy gasoline, is looking at ways to keep the warm feeling from turning chilly. Next year's design is a secret, Mr. Tursi said, but it has already been chosen so that Hess can start making more vehicles earlier to avert another sellout.

Hess may have a hard time. A postal worker from Brooklyn, who was leaving the Hess station at 10th Avenue in Manhattan last week with a bag of three police cars, said he had been buying multiples at the stations since the early 1970's.

"I have every one since 1964," he said. The most he ever spent was $2,300 at a toy fair for a 1967 velvet box truck. He spoke on the condition that his mother-in-law not find out.

And one station manager in New Jersey, who also insisted on anonymity, said he advised his regular customers two weeks ago to show up at 10 the next morning, when the delivery truck would arrive with the toys. The truck pulled in right on time — and so did 25 drivers who had followed it from the warehouse.

THE NEW YORK TIMES 12/15/93

collectors and toy dealers from absorbing large quantities. It is truly remarkable that with only 480 Company-owned service stations and 50 to 60 franchised stations, Hess sells almost two million toy trucks in three weeks. In 1995, over 600,000 toy truck promotionals were sold in the first three days alone.

Painstaking design and manufacturing standards deserve additional comment here. In recent years, some 24 different steel molds were used to cast each toy. The industry average is 12 molds. Again, this demonstrates the fine detailing found only in Hess toys.

No detail is overlooked. Everything must operate smoothly and correctly. All Hess colors and logos must be exact and approved by Hess. Many models, including the much sought after Hess Voyager, are said to be designed after a real vehicle in the Hess fleet. From early designs to the latest releases, I have seen many trucks on highways in the Northeast that mirror the miniature toys on my shelves at home. I will always remember seeing the Hess GMC Training Van. Two of these existed during the 1970's. They were used for on-site training for service station employees.

NEW HESS TANKER: The Hess Voyager is readied for launching ceremonies today at the Sparrows Point, Md., shipyard of Bethlehem Steel Company. The Voyager, first new tanker to be built from keel up for Hess Oil & Chemical Corporation, Perth Amboy, was sponsored by Mrs. Leon Hess, wife of Hess Oil's president. A supertanker of 48,500 tons deadweight, it will add 395,000 barrels of carrying capacity to the five-ship Hess fleet.

HESS ANNUAL REPORT
The USS Hess Voyager is launched

With each new year and toy comes a growing number of collectors, driving prices of earlier vehicles to record levels. A current year vehicle seems to double in price soon after inventories are depleted. At many antique and toy shows, I have witnessed price escalation on each vehicle with the early toys commanding a premium price. And, of course, models produced just once and not reissued benefit from the more limited edition value.

Also, special vehicles like the Hess Fire Pumper with water cannon, manufactured in 1970, and the 1986 and 1989 Ladder Trucks (each different) have captured the eye of specialty collectors. Same goes for boat collectors who seek out the 1966 Hess Voyager, to date the only non-land vehicle in the entire Hess collection with the exception of the 1995 Helicopter.

In 1982, Hess came out with a 1933 Chevy Fuel Oil Truck said to be a replica of the vehicle driven by Leon Hess when he was a young man in the fuel oil delivery business. The original truck sits on display at the Hess Oil Refinery in St. Croix, Virgin Islands. We will talk in detail about each model on the following pages.

All of the early Hess promotionals were manufactured by the Louis Marx Toy Company in the British Crown Colony of Hong Kong. The last year a Marx Toy logo appeared on a Hess toy vehicle was 1971. About this time, the Quaker Oats Company acquired the Marx Toy Company. At this point, Hess decided to produce the toys themselves, using an outside consulting company based in New York.

From 1964 to 1986, all Hess promotionals were manufactured in Hong Kong. The 1966 Hess Voyager and the 1967 Red Velvet Tanker were marked on the box "Made in the United States." This I have learned is not true. The mechanicals or film for the boxes were produced in the USA, but they were sent to Hong Kong for printing. The toys and the boxes were actually manufactured in Hong Kong and then shipped to the USA. Over the years, some injection samples were made in Hong Kong and then sent to the USA for final assembly and approval. The two I know of are the 1970 Fire Pumper and the 1975 Barrel Truck. Both are rare pieces and sought after by the specialty collector. In 1987, Hess, having to source out some of its production due to increased sales and costs, ordered 10 percent of its production to be made in China. The following year, 1988, roughly half of the toy trucks were made in China. Finally, in 1989, Hess was satisfied with the quality and moved the entire production to China where it remains today.

Production figures were usually kept confidential in the early years, but sources tell me that as little as 150,000 toy trucks were manufactured in 1964 and 1965. As demand increased

Hess' promotion on the fast track

In 1964, Leon Hess of the Hess Oil empire decided to sell a holiday promotional tanker truck at his gasoline stations.

And pretty much every year since then, Hess has offered a promotional toy at Christmastime. But if you wanted one this season, it's probably already too late.

Hess had a run on its $11.99 promotional patrol car that went on sale Thanksgiving Day. Last Friday, the company pulled its advertising for the holiday promotion, just eight days after the spots started airing.

In fact, Hess has sold nearly all the 1.5 million cars it produced for its 550 stations, and by Wednesday just a handful of stations on Long Island, in New Jersey and one on Tenth Ave. in Manhattan still had the cars.

Last year Hess ran out in mid-December, which is why it ordered 15% more toys this year.

"We have had unprecedented demand," said Carl Tursi, spokesman for New York-based Amerada Hess Corp. "We've been shipping and shipping, but by Friday a lot of the stations were already out."

The cars sold out so fast, Hess never got to air two of the three TV commercials it produced for the promotion.

In fact, while Hess may be king of the promotional road, it's now sharing the highway again, said Christopher Byrne, editor of Toy & Hobby World, an industry monthly.

"There's a lot of affection for these toys . . . A lot of kids got these toys in the Fifties and Sixties," said Byrne. "In just the last few years, they have made a comeback."

They have also become collector's items. For instance, the first Texaco promotional truck sold 10 years ago is now worth $900 on the collector's market, said Joby Humphrey, a spokeswoman for Star Enterprises, which markets Texaco products on the East Coast. She said this year's item, a diecast metal bank in the shape of a 1939 Dodge Airflo Texaco Truck is "selling like hot cakes."

But Hess is not pleased with the collectormania. The company is turning away upset customers with "sorry" signs posted at gas stations throughout the region. That's not exactly a way to promote good will among customers.

"We are not terribly happy about it (the collector's market). It isn't the reason for the promotion," said Tursi. He noted that next year, the company will increase production, and that it already is well into plans for '94 model.

HOT ITEM: The '93 version of Hess Oil's holiday promotion, a toy patrol car at $11.99, is nearly sold out already.

THE PITCH
Marketing & Advertising
PATRICIA WINTERS

THE DAILY NEWS 12/10/93

over the years and the word of quality and value spread throughout the East Coast, production soared to 1.3 million in 1992 and 1.5 million in 1993. A record two million toy trucks were produced in 1994 which failed to sell out, partially due to the unpopular design of the Hess Rescue Truck and the excessive quantity made.

The 1995 production was reduced back to 1.8 million units and, with an outstanding Hess Toy Truck and Helicopter combination, it completely sold out within three weeks. Before inventory was depleted, the Company even tried to warn its consumers with half page ads in local newspapers that the Truck and Helicopter were almost sold out. Hess, trying to reduce left over inventory from the previous year, began immediately delivering Rescue Trucks to their service stations as back up.

As you can read in the following magazine article, all Hess stories are not always happy. On Oct. 27/28, 1992, Hess reported a robbery in their warehouse in Woodbridge, NJ. A large quantity of valuable, older Hess toy trucks had been stolen. Many of us felt terrible about the loss to Hess doubting that the stolen

THE STAR LEDGER 12/7/93

trucks would ever be recovered. This article appeared in the 1992 Nov/Dec issue of *Toy Shop Magazine*, a trade publication for toys and collectibles. Not only were the toy trucks from Hess stolen, but many people often tried to profit by making bootleg knockoffs using Hess Company logos. Just recently, bogus underwater exploration vehicles and transformer rail cars have shown up at various toy shows, train shows and train stores. Hess vigorously defends their logo and trademarks in all cases, including one in 1993 when they sued a toy maker for producing tanker trucks bearing the Hess name and trademark green, yellow and white color schemes. Sold mostly in the Pennsylvania area as limited edition Hess Trucks, customers were being ripped off think-

HESS TOY TRUCKS

$5,000 REWARD

On October 27/28, 1992, a robbery occurred at the Amerada Hess Corporation warehouse facility in Woodbridge, New Jersey. A quantity of Hess toy trucks were stolen. This incident is being investigated by the Federal Bureau of Investigation and the Woodbridge Police Department.

Amerada Hess Corporation is hereby establishing a reward in the amount of $5,000 for information leading to the recovery of the stolen trucks.

Amerada Hess Corporation will be the sole judge of the person or persons (if more than one) entitled to the reward or any portion of it.

Any person having any information is urged to contact FBI Special Agent Robert DeBellis at (201) 622-5613, Sergeant David Bobal of Woodbridge Police Department at (908) 634-7700 or Joseph A. Dileo, Manager, Internal Affairs, Amerada Hess Corporation at (908) 750-6000.

TOY SHOP NOV/DEC 1992

COURTS

Gas firm claims toy maker doesn't want to play fair

■ Company says Lambertville manufacturer is making 'knock-offs' of the Hess trucks.

THE COURIER NEWS

ing they were buying a rare Hess truck when in truth they were buying an off-the-shelf toy with illegal logos and a new paint job.

Another warning and caution to Hess toy buyers. Many unethical dealers have sold 1986 Hess Fire Trucks charging ridiculously high prices for them claiming the bumpers and trim were gold plated by the Hess Company and sold as limited editions. Totally untrue! But many people were led down the primrose path with this story. In fact, it was a bad chrome plating job and poor quality control at the China factory. These trucks are actually worth less than a mint-in-box 1986 Fire Truck.

There are many totally unfounded stories about certain years of Hess trucks such as variations of wiring and switches that are supposed to indicate a difference in years. Let's not forget that these toys are basically hand-assembled and hand-made with multiple factories in China producing them. There will always be slight variations of injection colors, wiring, switches and small details. However, this should not escalate or devalue the price of that particular year. Many toy and collectible dealers dream up these small differences to inflate the value of their trucks.

As of this writing, there are officially 29 vehicles issued in the Hess Toy Collection, including the two models that were never sold publicly — the Amerada Hess Truck of 1969 and the Premium Diesel Truck of 1993. This figure does not include a vehicle that was made in two different countries or small variations occurring because of production facilities abroad.

Before I describe each toy in detail, I would like to thank Mr. Leon Hess and all the people of Amerada Hess Corp. of Woodbridge, NJ, (renamed in 1969) for designing, creating, and delivering these wonderful holiday presents for all to enjoy.

Michael V. Harwood 1996

Hess Oil Pumping Well

During 1961, an oil well pumping toy was produced by a Florida-based company. They were used by oil companies to promote sales, using company logos and trademarks. A few of these toys were purchased by Hess as a possible promotional item. This program was never implemented by Hess, who chose to go with a toy truck program instead. These oil wells are extremely rare and valuable.

1964 and 1965

The first of the Hess series appeared in 1964. Designed after a B-61 Mack tanker truck, it is painted in the old Company colors of dark green and white with bright yellow accents. This now rare tanker sold for $1.39 battery included. It was manufactured by Louis Marx and Company and is clearly marked "Made In Hong Kong by Marx Toy Company" underneath the truck. Uniquely designed, you can fill the tanker with water using the enclosed funnel, then empty it through its attached delivery hose. Measuring 12 1/2 inches, the vehicle has working head and tail lights operated by a switch at the rear of the tractor. Decals on the tanker display the name "Hess, Solvents and Chemicals, Fuel Oils and Gasoline" and a Hess Company logo appears on the bright red plastic funnel. Its colorful box, decorated with refinery and service station scenes, is silk-screened in the traditional Hess green, white and yellow and is also marked "Made In Hong Kong." The bottom half of the box is solid green. On the top and side of the box, it clearly states that this is an "Authentically Styled Miniature of the Hess Tank Trailer" from "America's Fastest Growing Integrated Oil Company." The box contains detailed instructions neatly placed inside showing how to operate the vehicle. Unique in design as well as the first toy of the collection, this tanker is rare and hard to find. It was reissued in 1965 with the cab molded in yellow plastic instead of green plastic for ease of painting the fenders.

1964 and 1965

23

1966

The holiday season of 1966 brought a very rare and special toy from the Hess Company — an outstanding replica of a Hess tanker ship, "The Hess Voyager." The model sold for $1.89 and features working white bow and stern lights, and red and green port and starboard lights operated by a switch on the deck of the ship. Even though the ship is equipped with roller wheels for land use, it may also be used in water (however, this is not recommended). "Hess Voyager" appears on the sides and stern of the ship and Hess Company logos on the smoke stack. The finely detailed ship measures 18 inches in length and includes very delicate anchors and propellers plus a flag on the stern. The multicolored, extremely attractive box is silk-screened with pictures of Hess Oil Company facilities and home delivery scenes. The box states, "Made in USA," but only the mechanicals for the box were made in the States. The actual ship and the box were made in the British Crown Colony of Hong Kong. The enclosed instructions and box bottom are colored in blue. A stand was also available, but did not come with the toy. The Voyager has become one of the most desirable pieces of the Hess collection because it was issued only once and was the only non-land vehicle sold until 1995. It is difficult to find in mint-in-box condition.

NOTE: "Made in U.S.A." on box

NOTE: Delicate flag and prop on stern and the U.S.A. decal

1966

1967

This year's toy brought a clean new look for the Tanker Truck — a split window tractor pulling a streamlined fuel oil tanker. An eighteen wheeler measuring 13 1/2 inches and painted in the traditional dark green with white and yellow accents, it reads, "Fuel Oils" on one side of the trailer and "Gasoline" on the other. Hess Company logo decals are on the rear of the trailer as well as the tractor doors. Although outfitted with a removable hose, this tanker cannot be filled with water like the earlier model. Working head and tail lights operate by a switch underneath the tanker. The truck itself was not marked underneath by Marx, but the box states, "Made in the U.S.A." Again only the mechanicals for the box were made in the States and then sent to Hong Kong, where the tanker and its box were manufactured and assembled. The toy sold for $1.99 and comes featured in a unique box lined with red velvet on the bottom half, clearly intended for display purposes. A card inside tells the owner, "The battery is already installed for your convenience" and further states, "Hess is known for service...If damaged in transit, return for replacement to the Hess Station where it was purchased." The top of the box is silk-screened in Hess colors depicting the truck and Hess service station scenes. This 1967 promotional, often referred to as the "Red Velvet Box," is one of the rarest toys in the collection, and now has become the hardest toy vehicle in the collection to find in excellent condition.

Note: "Made in U.S.A." on box end and red velvet trim.

1967

1968 and 1969

In 1968 and 1969, Hess reissued the 1967 Tanker Truck. The Marx Toy Company logo now appeared on the battery box cover beneath the tanker. It reads, "Made In Hong. Marx Toys." The toy sold for $1.49 and features a newly designed bottom half of the box. Gone is the red velvet, replaced by a basic white bottom. The top and sides of the box carry silk-screened pictures of the tanker as well as service station renderings. The end of the box reads, "Made in Hong Kong" and "Hess Oil and Chemical Corp Home Office Perth Amboy, New Jersey." The toy is 13 1/2 inches in length with working head and tail lights operated by a switch on the bottom of the tanker. As a collector, to make sure you have a 1968 or 1969 model, check the end of the box. In 1969 the words "Woodbridge, N.J." replaced "Perth Amboy." An instruction card was not included for either the 1968 or 1969 toy truck.

1968 Perth Amboy, N.J.

1969 Woodbridge, N.J.

1968 and 1969

1969...A Company Name Change

During 1969, the Hess Oil and Chemical Corporation merged with Amerada Petroleum Corporation. The new name became the Amerada Hess Corporation. The Hess Oil and Chemical Company became a division. The new company name appears on a Hess Oil Tanker Truck, the same model reissued in 1968/1969, but with wording on both the sides and rear of the tanker changed to read "Amerada Hess." The Hess Company logos disappeared on the cab doors, but the "Gasoline" decal on the right side and the "Fuel Oil" decal on the left side stayed. "Made In Hong Kong" is stamped on the battery box cover with the Marx Toy logo. The truck came in a completely new silk-screened box with two full length pictures of the toy and a rear view of the tanker on the back flap supporting the name "Amerada Hess." This truck was not sold at the service stations and was not available to the general public. It was an in-house promotion to announce the new company name and given to employees in the exploration and production areas of the company. If obtainable at all, it has to be one of the rarest in the collection.

1969
A Company Name Change

1970

In 1970, Hess produced a real Christmas surprise — a brilliant red, detailed replica of their fire engine used at the Port Reading , NJ, refinery. The truck is a pumper with two detachable rubber hoses on one side and a detachable ladder on the other. Glamorized by an abundant amount of chrome, the Fire Truck includes a swivelling, easily broken water cannon on the top. The pumper sold for $1.69 and features unique, realistic wheels with the tires clearly marked "Amerada Hess," but does not have working head and tail lights. Instead, a battery-operated, red emergency light flashes and rotates on the top of the cab. The completely chromed under chassis bears the stamp "Louis Marx and Company Inc. Made In Hong Kong" and the date in Roman Numerals "MCMLXX" (1970). This was one of the last toys ever to be produced under Louis Marx and Co. label. Eleven inches long, the pumper comes neatly packed with instructions for care and operation. The box features silk-screened pictures of the pumper and Hess facilities and reads, "Hess Oil and Chemical Division, Amerada Hess Corporation" on one end. I consider this toy one of the finest pieces created by the Hess Company and another hard one to acquire. Specialty collectors again seek this toy, making it extremely scarce and valuable.

1970

1971 Seasons Greetings

The winter of 1971 brought back the 1970 Fire Truck. This year's pumper again sold for $1.69 and was exactly the same toy. Sometime during the holiday season, the Company ran out of the colorful silk-screened boxes and issued the toy in a plain white box that reads "Seasons Greetings" across the top. This box is very difficult to find which makes it extremely valuable.

1971
Seasons
Greetings

1972 and 1974

In 1972 and again in 1974, Hess reissued the 1968 Tanker Truck. (In 1973, they offered no promotional toy most likely due to oil increases and overall poor economic conditions.) Selling for $1.69 and $1.89 respectively, the only noticeable difference between these two models and the 1968/69 version can be found in a slight color variation and in the exhaust stacks. The later trucks are injected in lighter green and have shorter stacks, probably to avoid breakage. Another easy way to differentiate between the vehicles is that the 1968 and 1969 trucks have square trailer feet, and the 1972/74 have round trailer feet. The box itself remains the same as the previous tanker in 1968/69 with one exception — the end flap states, "Amerada Hess Corporation." Again there was not an instruction card issued in either 1972 or 1974.

'72 & '74 '68 & '69
NOTE: Exhaust stacks and box ends

'72 & '74 '68 & '69
NOTE: Trailer feet and plastic color

1972 and 1974

1975

The holiday season of 1975 brought a newly designed cab and handsome Box Trailer, an excellent replica of trucks then seen on East Coast highways making deliveries to service stations. The cab features a one piece windshield with chrome accessories. Sliding doors on each side of the uniquely designed Box Trailer open to reveal a battery compartment in an on-board pallet. Rear doors on the trailer also open and close. The truck sold for $1.99. Measuring 14 inches and painted in traditional Hess colors, it rolls along on black rubber tires authentically marked "Amerada Hess" and has colorful red wheels and bumpers. Inside the Box Trailer are carefully packed three miniature oil drums. Once again, the toy features working head and tail lights operated by a switch underneath the trailer. It is stamped, "Made In Hong Kong" and "Amerada Hess Corporation" on the bottom of the trailer. The white box, silk-screened in green, yellow and red, pictures Hess service stations and the truck itself. A small instruction card tucked inside the box explains where and how to install the battery. A thoroughly enjoyable toy, this promotional barrel and Box Trailer Truck from Hess is a sought after piece in the collection.

1975

HESS
RS
HESS

HESS
OIL & CHEMICAL CO.
HESS
HESS
TRUCK
ENTRANCE

1976

Here again Hess reissued the 1975 Box Trailer and barrel truck. To the casual observer, it looks the same, but a closer look reveals some changes from the previous year. The removable miniature oil barrels returned. However, this year Hess logos appeared on the drums. The cab itself underwent a very interesting, although hard to notice, change. The 1975 cab came from a one piece mold instead of the two piece mold used in 1976, most likely to eliminate the process of masking and hand painting the fenders. The color of the 1976 truck is a much darker green. And the price was $2.29, an increase brought on, no doubt, by inflation. The enclosed instruction card remains the same. On the 1976 box, the words "Made In Hong Kong" were added to the end flap. A caution clearly marked on the box for both years states, " Due to small parts, not recommended for children under three years old." The avid collector should have both model years because of these significant changes.

1976 1975

NOTE: Split cab on 1976, also "Made in Hong Kong" was added to the end flap on box.

1976

1977

The holiday season of 1977 again brought a new detailed version of a Hess Fuel Oil Tanker. Painted in the traditional dark green and white with yellow accents, this year's tanker glistens with added chrome on the cab, bright red wheels and tires clearly marked with "Amerada Hess." The toy comes with working head and tail lights operated by a switch underneath the tanker. Reading "Fuels Oils" on one side and "Gasoline" on the other, Hess Company logo decals are on the front doors of the cab and rear of the tanker. This vehicle sold for $2.39 and measures 13 1/2 inches in length. The battery box cover reads, "Amerada Hess Corporation. Made in Hong Kong," with the Roman numerals "MCMLXXVII" (1977). The colorful box has typical silk-screened pictures of the tanker and a Hess service station. An enclosed card provides battery installation and operating instructions. This truck is a very neat and worthy toy and should appreciate quickly in the collection.

1977

45

1978

Winter of 1978 brought a reissue of the 1977 Fuel Oil Tanker. The price this year rose to $2.49 and, as always, includes a battery. The date on the battery cover still reads "MCMLXXVII. (1977) Made in Hong Kong." The only way I have found to distinguish the 1977 model from the 1978 is by the Hess Company logo labeled on the back of the tanker. In 1977, the rear logo measures 1 1/2 inches long by 1 inch high. Also the "Hess" lettering itself is flatter and longer. Dimensions of the 1978 model are 1 1/2 inches long by 7/8 of an inch high with bolder and taller "Hess" lettering. The box, silk-screened the same in both years, also includes an instruction card. Distinguishing between the almost identical models can be challenging, but both models are a must for the serious collector.

1978

1977 1978

1980

In 1979, Hess did not sell a promotional toy probably due to the economic conditions in the U.S. Then in 1980, a totally new design came out — the Hess Training Van. It is a GMC motor home replica of the vehicle Hess used to conduct field training seminars at Hess service stations along the East Coast. This very realistic toy van has an operating side door, pop-up TV antenna, and, of course, operating head and tail lights controlled by a switch underneath. Unique to the Training Van are its fully detailed interior and the tasteful use of chrome on accessories like hubcaps, bumpers, sideview mirrors and windshield wipers. Measuring 11 1/2 inches and molded in overall white with dark green accent stripes, the van is silk-screened on the side with the company name, logo, and type of vehicle. Commercial New Jersey license plates on front and back add a further touch of realism. Engraved in the plastic underneath the van, it states, "Amerada Hess Corporation" and "Made In Hong Kong" with a date "Copyright 1978." It sold for $3.29 and included batteries and operating instructions. Until now Hess always packed their trucks in a two piece cake style box. This newly designed one-piece bright green box, silk-screened with four pictures of the van, is marked in bright yellow at the top, "Hess Training Van." Extremely tightly packed, care has to be taken not to destroy the chrome sideview mirrors when pulling the van in and out of the box. The training van is becoming a rare, hard to find piece of the collection and is one of my favorites. In 1981, again no promotional vehicle was sold.

1980

HESS
TRAINING VAN
gasoline station personnel
AMERADA HESS CORPORATION
CAUTION!
DUE TO SMALL PARTS, NOT RECOMMENDED FOR CHILDREN UNDER 3 YEARS OLD.
HESS
TRAINING VAN
AMERADA HESS CORPORATION

1982 and 1983

The Hess Company really outdid themselves in 1982 with a totally realistic model of a 1933/34 Chevrolet Fuel Oil Delivery Truck. This newly designed "work of art" is not a tractor trailer truck, but a six wheel straight truck. It features a rubber oil delivery hose that pulls out of the side and easily rewinds back on its spool. Other authentic touches include "Hess" raised-letter tires, black rubber foot treads under the cab doors, which actually open, and working head and tail lights operated by a switch located underneath the truck. For a special old-fashioned flair, it even has an open style windshield. A New Jersey license plate marked "Commercial 1933" attaches to a red front bumper. The truck is dark green with white and yellow accents. The overall length is 11 inches and it sold for $4.69 including battery. The truck is marked underneath with the words "Made in Hong Kong. MCMLXXX (1980). Amerada Hess Corporation." This is the truck said to be a copy of the original delivery tanker driven by Leon Hess when he was a young man in the fuel oil delivery business. The one piece box features colored silk-screened pictures of the tanker on each side, neatly framed in gold, with the name "The First Hess Truck" written in gold on the top of the box. For the first time, the detailed operating instructions come clearly printed on the bottom of the box. This good old-fashioned toy truck, a favorite among many collectors, has increased in price accordingly. The exact same truck was issued at the service stations in 1983.

1982 and 1983

1984

The first savings bank issued by Hess arrived for Christmas of 1984, a redesigned version of the 1977/78 Fuel Oil Tanker. This new function marked the beginning of a whole new series of Hess promotions. This wonderful toy savings bank with a coin slot on the rear tanker allows you to access your savings by turning the last cap on the tanker. Although the truck retains the overall dark green and white and yellow accents, most of the yellow trim around the Company logos and other labels disappeared. Working head and tail lights still operate by the familiar switch underneath the trailer. Clearly marked, the battery cover again states, "Amerada Hess Corporation. Made In Hong Kong." Only this time the Roman numerals read "MCMLXXXIV" (1984). A one piece box introduced the Tanker Truck Bank with two pictures of the toy and shows a small child's hand inserting a coin into the slot. Colored instructions not only appear on the bottom of the box, but there's also a separate card packed inside with duplicate instructions for the bank compartment. The truck originally sold for a bargain price of $4.99, including battery. Although similar to the 1977 and 1978 Fuel Oil Tanker, it's a treasured year in everyone's collection due to its bank feature.

1984

HESS
FUEL OILS
HESS
CAUTION!
Due to small parts, not recommended for children under three years old.
HESS
FUEL OILS

1985

For the holiday season in 1985, Hess brought back the 1982/83 issue of the 1933 Chevy, but they smartly converted the tanker into a savings bank. Named "First Hess Truck Bank," its center storage tank holds a unique coin slot and can be opened by turning a knob to access the coins. Identically marked underneath and still reading "MCMLXXX" (1980) in Roman numerals, everything remains unchanged except for the silk-screening on the box. New pictures of the old-fashioned tanker truck driving through a snow-covered countryside show a little child's hand inserting a quarter in the slot. Detailed directions on the bottom of the box explain how to install the battery and work the bank compartment. The truck sold for $3.99. Surprisingly, geographic location determined which toy was sold. In the North, we received the 1985 '33 Chevy bank, but the South received the 1984 Hess Tanker bank again. This must have been a way for Hess to reduce inventories at their warehouse. Both versions of the 1933 Chevy Fuel Oil Delivery Trucks are valued pieces and still quite obtainable.

1985

HESS
GASOLINE
HESS
CAUTION!
Due to small parts, not recommended for children under 3 years old.

1986

The 1986 holiday heralded the arrival of a newly designed fire truck. The red "Toy Fire Truck Bank" brightens the eyes of children and collectors alike because of its multi-functions and features including flashing dome lights, and head and tail lights operated by separate switches. It features a working aerial ladder with three sections that completely swivel and a coin slot neatly concealed under the ladder. Operating chrome feet pull down to stabilize the toy when the ladder is fully extended. Detailed chrome abundantly adorns all sides of the fire truck including the front bumper and sideview mirrors. Stamped on the bottom of the truck, it reads, "Amerada Hess Corporation. Made In Hong Kong," with Roman numerals "MCMLXXXVI" (1986). The black chassis is also detailed with the "Hess" name on the authentic black rubber tires, even the spare. Hess deserves high praise on the design and detail of this magnificent truck. Measuring 12 3/4 inches, it sold for $5.49 including batteries. The beautiful one piece box pictures the truck parked in New York City at night with the Rockefeller Center Christmas tree sparkling in the background. Instructions for the special feature once again appear silk-screened on the bottom. The Toy Fire Truck Bank will, in my opinion, be a fast rising star in the Hess collection and is already becoming hard to find.

1986

HESS
HESS
CAUTION:
Due to small parts, not recommended for children under 3 years of age.
HESS

1987

Clean, white and new best describe the 1987 Hess promotional toy. The freshly designed 18 Wheel Tractor Trailer is a box truck bank with oil barrels. The truck's totally new, plain paint scheme resembles the clean white image of the Hess service station. The tractor trailer is molded in overall white with light green trim and plenty of chrome. A new front end includes chrome doorsteps, exhaust stacks, horns, sideview mirrors and all the trim on the trailer. Three miniature green oil barrels come wrapped separately. The familiar undercarriage switch that operates the head and tail lights also operates newly added clearance and running lights. The truck has sliding cargo doors and a coin slot on top of the trailer for the bank. The rear trailer door opens by a red knob to withdraw your savings. All the Hess Company logos and labeling are done in light green. Gone are the traditional yellow accents. The overall length of the toy is 14 1/4 inches and it sold for $5.99 including the battery. "Amerada Hess Corporation. "Made In Hong Kong" or "Made in China" is stamped on the battery box cover with the date "MCMLXXXVII" (1987). A stunning one piece box is silk-screened with a picture of the truck driving through the snow-covered countryside at night passing a small frozen pond. Ice skaters and lighted trees accent the holiday spirit. The top of the box reads "Hess Toy Truck Bank" and has detailed instructions on the bottom for installing the battery and working the bank compartment. The end of the box can read "Made In Hong Kong" or "Made In China." Only 10% of the total production was made in China, making this version worth more and harder to find.

1987

HESS
GASOLINE
LS
HESS
GASOLINE
FUEL OILS
CAUTION: Due to small parts, not recommended for children under 3 years of age.

1988

"The Toy Truck and Racer" made its grand appearance in 1988. This promotional from Hess features a friction powered toy car that resembles a formula style racer on the rear of the trailer. The car can be detached and used as a separate toy. The tractor portion remains basically the same as 1987, but Hess removed the spoiler from the top, added an air conditioner compressor, and changed the chrome exhaust stack. The race car trailer itself is unique and detailed, including a well hidden battery storage compartment in the supply section at the front of the trailer. The Truck and Racer are molded in the new Hess colors, overall white with light green trim. Authentic chrome wheels and Hess lettered tires plus lots of other chrome accent the toy. The Truck measures 12 inches and the Racer 4 3/4 inches. The toy sold for $6.95 including battery. A switch underneath the trailer operates the head and tail lights as well as yellow running and clearance lights. Among many unique features, and probably important to all collectors, is the date on the rear license plate. This is the first year Hess added the date to the plate, making it easy for all to identify. The bottom of the race car and the truck are clearly marked "Amerada Hess Corporation. Made In China" or "Made In Hong Kong" with the date "MCMLXXXVIII" (1988). The colorful silk-screened box shows a truck and racer parked at the Hess station during the holiday season with snow-capped mountains in the background. "Hess Toy Truck and Racer" is written in red on top of the box and detailed instructions on the bottom show operations of the racer and battery installation. The end of the box either reads "Made In China" or "Made In Hong Kong." Approximately 50% of the toys were manufactured in China and the other 50% in Hong Kong.

1988

HESS
GASOLINE
HESS
HESS
GASOLINE
CAUTION: Due to small parts, not recommended for children under 4 years of age

1989

Christmas 1989 brought a great surprise. Hess reissued the 1986 Fire Truck and added several interesting features. For the first time, Hess introduced sound to their toy — a unique dual sound siren operated by a separate switch — making it a wonderful addition for children and collectors alike. Instead of red, the new Fire Truck is molded white with light green trim, and the aerial ladder is now red instead of white. Other features include working head and tail lights and emergency flashers operated by another switch underneath. Slight changes to the actual plastic sides are easily noticed. The license plate on the back states 1989. This toy truck is also a savings bank. It measures 12 3/4 inches long and sold for $8.99 including batteries. Underneath it's marked, "Amerada Hess Corporation. Made In China. MCMLXXXIX" (1989). The one piece box has a picture of the Fire Truck parked at a Hess service station during the holiday season. Snow-capped mountains and brightly lighted Christmas trees compliment the scene. Written in red and green on the top of the box, it states, "Hess Toy Fire Truck" and on the bottom the detailed installations and operation instructions appear. The entire production of this truck was made in China. This finely detailed Fire Truck is readily available. It's not only a must for everyone's collection, but it would be a greater delight to have all three fire truck models - 1970, 1986, and 1989.

1989

1990

The 1990 holiday season, Hess brought out a newly designed rugged toy Tanker Truck — the most sturdy piece in the entire collection so far. This beautiful gasoline tanker, molded in overall white with light green trim, carries the "Hess" name numerous times in light green on the truck. Worth mentioning are the tanker truck's 36 working lights — red, yellow and white headlights, tail lights and running lights. In addition to the familiar light switch that operates all those lights, this totally new tanker has an added three-way switch underneath to activate a horn and a backup alert. Chrome adorns the wheels, bumpers, gas tank and accessories. A license plate attached to the rear bumper reads, "Hess 1990." The battery compartment is located underneath stamped with the words "Amerada Hess Corporation. Made In China. MCMXC" (1990). The truck is 15 inches long and sold for $9.99 including batteries. The one piece box features the truck at night parked in front of a Hess service station during the holiday season with snow flurries just starting to fall to give us the warm Christmas feeling. The top of the box marked in green and red lettering states, "Hess Toy Tanker Truck" and "Dual Sound Switch." The bottom of the box again gives instructions for installing batteries and operating the sound and light switches. This toy sold out very quickly due partly to its value, beautiful design and childproof ruggedness — not to mention being a spectacular addition for the collector.

1990

65

1991

Thanksgiving Day, 1991, we were off to the races again. The Hess Race Car theme surfaced this year, as it did in 1988. This toy has great eye appeal for the collector and, in keeping with Hess tradition of building fine toys, has lasting durability. The 1991 Hess Toy Truck and Racer was priced at $10.99 and included two alkaline batteries to power the illuminated logos and the vehicle's 27 white, amber and red lights. The toy Race Car, resembling a Lamborghini, is friction powered and marked "Amerada Hess Corp. Made In China. MCMXCI" (1991) on the bottom. Measuring 12 inches long and 3 3/4 inches high, the truck is molded in white and accented with traditional Hess green. Red wheels and liberal chrome attachments greatly enhance this toy. The noticeable differences between the 1988 truck and the 1991 model are mainly in the cab portion. The battery enclosure is unique for 1991, being located at the rear of the trailer in the carrying deck while the operating switch remains on the bottom of the trailer. For easy identification both car and trailer carry "Hess 1991" rear license plates. The silk-screened box depicts a snowy Christmas scene with the truck parked by a busy Hess Gasoline and Service Mart. The battery installation and Toy Racer operating instructions remain on the bottom of the box. This Hess Toy Truck and Racer prove again the ruggedness and collectibility of these fine toys from our friends at Amerada Hess.

1991

HESS
GASOLINE
HESS
HESS
GASOLINE
HESS
Seasons Greetings
HESS MART
HESS
GASOLINE
HESS

67

1992

Autumn of 1992 brought a new concept in transportation. The Hess 18 Wheeler and Racer offered by Hess gas stations Thanksgiving Day was a huge success. It was reported by some stations that the toys sold out in hours. This year's toy features a tractor trailer truck with loading ramp transporting a race car seen through a unique, lighted open window in the trailer. As always, two alkaline batteries are included in the $11.99 price. This 18 Wheeler is 15 inches long and 3 3/4 inches high and features 31 white, red, and yellow lights. For easy identification, "Hess 1992" appears on the rear license plate of both trailer and racer. Batteries are neatly concealed in the bottom of the trailer alongside the operating switch. Markings on the bottom read, "Copyright 1992. Amerada Hess Corporation. Made in China." This year's Race Car, resembling a Porsche, is friction powered. For the first time, a watch battery operated the car lights. An instruction card has been included for the operation of the racer lights and for the replacement of the battery. Following a trend from 1987, the toy is molded in white and accented with traditional Hess green. The attractive one piece box has multi-color bold letters "Hess 18 Wheeler and Racer" on top. Pictured on both sides is the Truck and Racer parked by a Hess Mart on a snowy winter's eve. Battery and ramp instructions are located on the box bottom. Children and collectors alike agree that the Hess 18 Wheeler will be a favorite. This new design concept illustrated one more time Amerada Hess' continuing commitment to building superior, collectible toys.

1992

69

1993

Lights flashing and sirens blaring woke us all on Thanksgiving morning, 1993, with yet another new concept in Hess promotionals. Designed more toward a younger child's market than usual, this uniquely styled Hess Patrol Car molded in overall white with green trim and Hess logos has a realistic sound chip and an advanced lighting system. The rear license plate clearly states "1993" for identification. Hess kept the price of $11.99 for 1993, and, of course, it included the alkaline batteries. Approximately 1.5 million Patrol Cars were produced and sold. Not bad considering its rather uncomplicated design. Hess' decision to increase production 15% over 1992 was due mainly to an increase in demand from satisfied consumers.The vehicle measures 10 1/2 inches in length and delivers in a color, silk-screened box depicting a Hess service station on a clear, cold winter holiday evening. Battery information is conveniently located on the bottom of its box. Although collectors weren't particularly pleased with the Patrol Car design due to lack of detail, it had little affect on its sales.

1993

HESS
GASOLINE
HESS
HESS
HESS
GASOLINE
WARNING: Contains small parts which may be hazardous to children under 4 years of age.

1993 Premium Diesel

A real plus to the Hess toy collector arrived shortly after Thanksgiving Day in 1993 — a Limited Edition Hess Premium Diesel, never intended to be sold in their service stations. This graphically changed version of a 1990 Hess Truck was distributed to bulk Premium Diesel customers and many friends of Mr. Hess as a gift. The rare truck arrived in a green, neatly gift wrapped box with a separate gift card. This truck exploded the Hess collection to a new level. I'm sure Hess never wanted this to happen. As I understand it, Hess would like to discourage the collector market. If so, this totally backfired. The price soared to a reported $2,200 and then declined to the $800 to $1,200 range. Eventually, I feel this price will rebound. We understand that 10,000 or more units were produced with initial distribution at about 6,000 gifts. This Premium Diesel Tanker Truck and the Amerada Hess Tanker Truck of 1969 are the only two promotionals that were not available to the general public from the Hess Company.

1993
Premium
Diesel

1994

Flashing lights and a loud siren best describe the 1994 Hess Rescue Truck. A bright red aerial ladder adorns this tow truck-styled vehicle. Chrome legs act as stabilizers on each side of the Rescue Truck along with the lengthy extension ladder. The Rescue Truck measures 10 inches in length and is molded in overall white with painted green trim and Company logos. Hess continues to identify the year it was manufactured with a license plate. The truck is packaged in a colorfully-illustrated, one piece box with instructions printed on the bottom. Hess raised the price nearly $3.00 per unit at the pumps to $14.95, probably due to higher plastic costs in China. A record 2.0 million were reportedly made and did not sell well at the service stations due to the overall poor design, lack of detail and the large quantity produced. This vehicle, apparently aimed at the younger market, reduced sales and left Hess burdened with leftover inventory. Resale value on this particular vehicle is the lowest of all the toys in the Hess collection.

1994

75

1995

Clearly regaining command of the toy promotional market in 1995, Hess fired back with one of their best vehicles to date — a remarkable high quality, delicately detailed Hess Toy Truck and Helicopter. This is one of only two non-land vehicles ever produced by Hess. In the first three days of sales, starting four days before Thanksgiving, Hess sold a record 600,000 units. To this date, no other petroleum company has even produced close to 600,000 plastic units, let alone sold them in just three days. For the first time, Hess released the trucks before Thanksgiving Day, making many customers happy not to fight waiting lines on the holiday. The truck itself measures 14 1/2 inches long and is molded again in white with the familiar painted green trim and Company logos. A removable Helicopter molded in the same colors comes with flashing lights and a rotating main rotor blade and rear spinning rotor. Batteries are included and already come installed in the Helicopter. Additional batteries are included for the numerous operating lights on the truck. A sliding ramp to off-load the chopper is neatly installed in the truck's trailer. Once again, the license plate reads "1995" for identification purposes. A total of 1.8 million toys were reportedly manufactured in China and completely sold out in three weeks at the 500 or more Hess service stations along the East Coast. The price increased $1.00 over the previous year to $15.99. Worth mentioning is the familiar, well designed, one piece color box with instructions printed on the bottom. I feel this truck will escalate in value at twice the rate of the preceding two years.

1995

HESS
GASOLINE
HESS
HESS
GASOLINE
HESS
HESS
HESS
GASOLINE
HESS
HESS
GASOLINE
WARNING:
CHOKING HAZARD-Small parts.
Not for children under 3 years.

History of Hess

Year	Vehicle	Original Cost
1964	B Mack (tank truck, with funnel)	$1.39
1965	B Mack (same as 1964)	$1.39
1966	Ship - (The Hess Voyager)	$1.89
1967	Tank Truck (new, with red velvet box)	$1.99
1968	Tank Truck (same as 1967, Perth Amboy, NJ)	$1.49
1969	Tank Truck (same as 1968, Woodbridge, NJ)	$1.49
1970	Fire Truck (red pumper with water cannon)	$1.69
1971	Fire Truck (red pumper same as 1970)	$1.69
1972	Tank Truck (same as 1968 with minor changes)	$1.69
1973	No promotion	
1974	Tank Truck (same as 1972)	$1.89
1975	Box Trailer (no Hess labels on oil drums, one piece cab)	$1.99
1976	Box Trailer (Hess labels on oil drums, two piece cab)	$2.29
1977	Tank Truck (new tractor trailer, rear label 1.5" long by 1" high)	$2.39
1978	Tank Truck (same as 1977, rear label 1.5" long by 7/8" high)	$2.49
1979	No promotion	

Promotional Toy Trucks

Year	Vehicle	Original Cost
1980	Training Van (GMC motor home)	$3.29
1981	No promotional	
1982/83	1933 Chevy Fuel Oil Delivery Truck	$4.69
1984	Tanker Truck Bank (first bank)	$4.99
1985	1933 Chevy Oil Truck Bank (North) Tank Truck Bank 1984 (South)	$3.99
1986	Fire Truck Bank (red)	$5.49
1987	18 Wheel Tractor Trailer (box truck with oil barrels)	$5.99
1988	Truck and Racer	$6.95
1989	Fire Truck Bank (white)	$8.99
1990	Tanker Truck (new)	$9.99
1991	Truck and Racer	$10.99
1992	18 Wheeler Truck and Racer	$11.99
1993	Patrol Car	$11.99
1994	Rescue Truck	$14.95
1995	Truck and Helicopter	$15.99

Collector Tips

The most desired condition in toy collecting is described as "Mint-in-Box" (MIB). Some of the features that qualify a toy for this condition are as follows:

1. All decals and labels should be original and attached.
2. All original parts and accessories must be included.
3. The box should be clean. No tears, blemishes or crushed ends.
4. All inserts and packing material, as well as the instruction card, should be inside.

Additional Tips

1. All these toys are made of plastic and warp easily. Keep them stored in a cool, dry place.
2. Keep the toy away from direct sunlight since the plastic and the box will discolor.
3. As of 1995, a complete collection consists of 29 vehicles.
4. With time and patience, an entire collection is still obtainable. (A prime reason why a Hess collection is gaining popularity).
5. Collectors should always obtain the new promotional toy when it is released each year, regardless if it is a re-issue. (Sometimes small changes are made either to the toy or the box.)

Where and How to Find Hess Promotional Toys

1. Antique and Toy Collectible dealers and stores
2. Flea markets
3. Antique Toy and Collectible shows
4. Local garage sales
5. Antique and Collectible newspapers and magazines
6. Local newspapers and magazines
7. Auctions
8. Computer on-line services (Internet and the World Wide Web)
9. Automotive and truck shows and swapmeets
10. Automotive auctions

Happy Collecting!

The Servco, Wilco Connection

During the period 1960 through 1965, Hess Oil and Chemical Corp. embarked on a rapid expansion program into new markets outside of their traditional sales area of NJ, NY, CT, PA, DE, and MD.

Hess began marketing gasoline through its own stations in August 1960, and by 1962 had 32 Hess stations in operation. Most of these were older gas stations purchased from other oil companies. These stations were cleaned up, rebuilt and rebranded with the Hess name. In addition, Hess supplied gasoline to approximately 250 service stations selling under the names Save-Way, Merit and Giant. Kerosene, #2 fuel oil, residual fuels, solvents, chemicals and gasoline were sold and delivered to its customers using the fleet of 250 Hess owned trucks. These vehicles with their distinctive green and white paint schemes became the most visible sign of the Hess operation on the East Coast in the early 60's. During this period, Hess also acquired, for the first time, crude oil production, pipelines, and an oil refinery

Entire fleet of Hess Trucks, Perth Amboy terminal (1952)

in Mississippi. Several large wholesale marketers on the East Coast were purchased and merged into the Hess marketing program.

Then a giant step was taken in 1963. Hess purchased Delhi Taylor Refining and marketing properties which included two oil refineries in Texas, deep water terminals, and terminals on the Plantation Pipeline System, as well as many contracts for gasoline, fuel oils, chemicals and petrochemicals customers. The Delhi purchase also provided Hess with an additional 110 gasoline stations marketing under several brand names, and a 35% stock interest in 150 "Billups" Service Stations.

Advertising material was prepared promoting the Hess name and its expanded fleet of over 400 transport trucks. During 1964, a plastic toy model of the Hess Tanker Truck was created to be used as a marketing tool and sent to all gasoline, fuel oil and petrochemical customers of the two companies. Additionally, a small number of Billups toy trucks were produced by Hess for the same reason.

During early 1965, Billups merged with Hess. Immediately Hess started changing the name on the Billups stations to the every-expanding Hess name. Many of these Billups stations had to be rebuilt or torn down to meet the Hess standards of a clean white service station image.

Later in 1965, toy trucks were also made available from Hess to their large volume gasoline customers in the Southeast, using their individual names. These toy trucks resembling a B-61 Mack Tanker bore the names Service, Wilco, Etna, Gant, McCoy, Travelers and Billups. A total of eight B-Macks were produced by Marx Toys using the Hess mold. Fewer than 5,000 each of these very rare toy tanker trucks were manufactured. Pictured here are the few I have seen.

Each year thereafter, as a new toy truck was introduced, Hess allowed its customers in North Carolina (Service and Wilco) to continue using its toy mold the year after Hess introduced it. The era of the Servco and Wilco toy trucks had begun.

From 32 service stations in 1962 to over 550 in 1995, Hess has sold over 20 million toy trucks. The following pages include the entire fleet of trucks Hess produced for Servco and Wilco.

Note: Service Distributing Company, Inc. (Servco). The name "Service" appeared on all the toy trucks from 1966 until 1976. Then, in 1979,

From the private collection of John P. Gulino

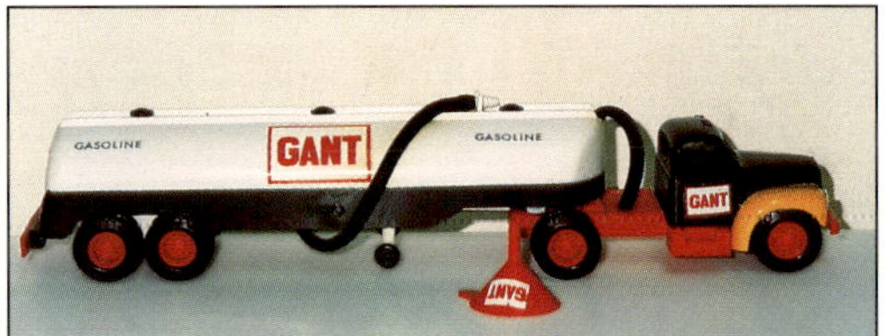

From the private collection of Douglas W. Campbell

"Service Plus" appeared on the side of their toy tanker. In 1986, "Servco" appeared on the toy promotional and has been the name ever since. Also, the color of their toy trucks changed five times in thirty years. Green, yellow and white in 1966 became blue and white in 1969, then red and white through the 1970's, followed by green and white in 1986, and finally back to the traditional red and white every year since then. The company today is still known as Service Distributing Company, based in Albemarle, North Carolina, but markets its gasoline through the Servco brand name. A total of fourteen holiday promotionals has been released in the series.

Note: A.T. Williams Oil Company (Wilco)

From headquarters in Winston-Salem, NC, the A.T. Williams Oil Company markets their gasoline through the Wilco brand name. The name "Wilco" has appeared on all toy truck promotionals since 1965. The company colors of blue and white have remained the same throughout the collection. A total of thirteen holiday promotionals has been released in the series.

SERVCO

1966

1967

SERVCO

1972

87

From the private collection of Douglas W. Campbell

1969

From the private collection of Douglas W. Campbell

SERVCO

1979

1976

SERVCO

1986

1989

89

SERVCO

1990

90

1991

SERVCO

1993

91

1992

SERVCO

1994

92

1995

FUEL OILS
GASOLINE
WILCO
SOLVENTS
CHEMICALS
WILCO

1966

1967

WILCO
WILCO

WILCO

1969

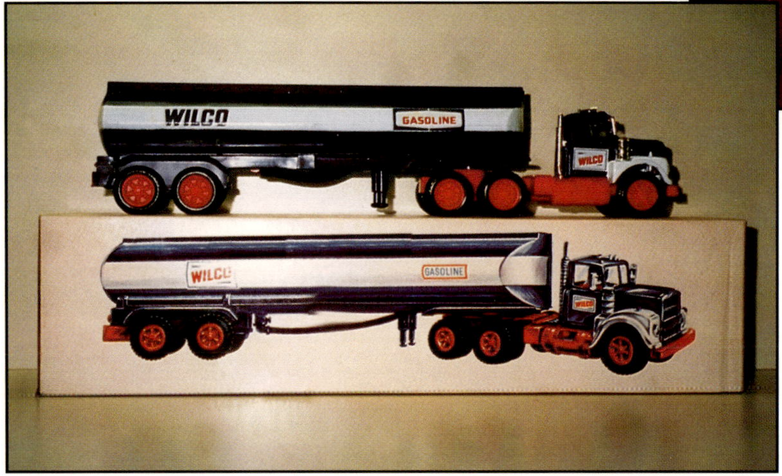

From the private collection of Douglas W. Campbell

1985

WILCO

1986

1988

95

WILCO

1989

1990

WILCO

1991

1992

WILCO

1993

98

1994

WILCO
GASOLINE
WARNING:
CHOKING HAZARD-Small parts.
Not for children under 3 years

1995

Special Trucks and Memorabilia

In 1969 Mr. Hess gave away a special gift wrapped truck. Now very rare, this Amerada Hess Truck is one of only two that was never sold to the general public.

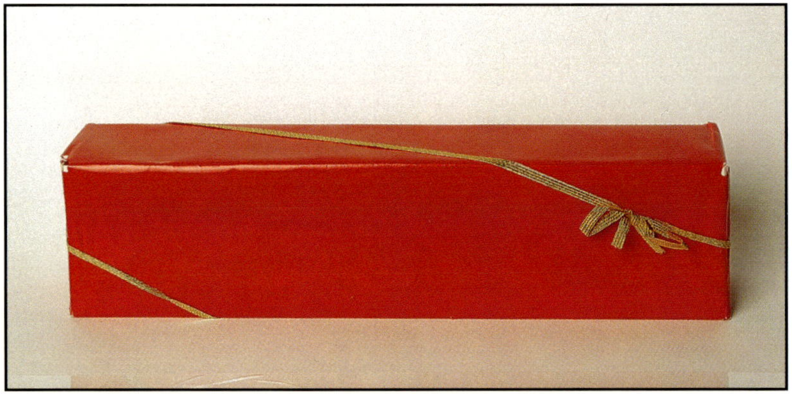

In 1993 Mr. Hess gave away another promotional gift. The Hess Premium Diesel Truck arrived in a bright green gift wrapped box. Again, this was never sold to the general public.

If you were fortunate enough to receive your 1964/1965 Hess Tanker by mail, this is how it arrived. A handy mail sleeve with a label attached concealed a regular station-issue Hess toy and box.

102

From the private collection of Douglas W. Campbell

A very rare Travelers Boat

Less than 5,000 each of these very rare Gant, Etna and Billups toy tanker trucks were produced by Hess in 1965. Hess made a total of eight different B-Mack toy models with funnels — Hess, Service, Wilco, Billups, Gant, Etna, McCoy and Travelers.

From the private collection of John P. Gulino

From the private collection of Douglas W. Campbell

Hess Buttons

1st Edition

1992

2nd Edition

1993

3rd Edition

1994

4th Edition

1995

In 1992, Hess produced the first button that attendants wore on their uniforms while the toy promotion was on sale. Every year since then, they have followed this tradition. Many collectors feel as I do that these unique 3 inch diameter buttons will become a desired and appreciating collectible as the program continues.

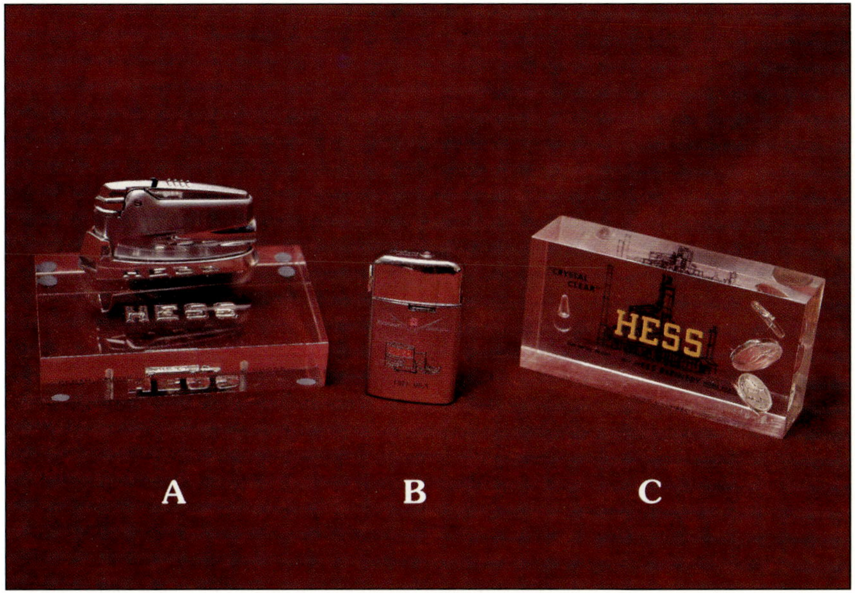

A. This high quality Ronson lighter with an aluminum holder mounted on a clear lucite base was issued in 1955 to approximately 200 fuel oil companies. The original Perth Amboy office phone number (Valley 6-1000) appeared along the bottom with a little white metal tanker truck engraved with the words Hess. The Hess name also appeared on the back of the lighter as well as on the base itself.

B. In 1959, another Ronson lighter was given to fifty or so customers who purchased propane produced at the Hess Port Reading Refinery. Pictured was a Hess storage tank, a ship and, of course, a tanker truck.

C. A clear acrylic block paper weight with the Port Reading Refinery scene in the background contained a sample drop of crystal clear home heating oil and three floating coins. The coins represented the profits that oil distributors would receive by selling Hess Heating Oils.

HESS TOY TRUCK GLASSES

COLLECTOR'S SERIES

Another new marketing 'first' has been created by Amerada Hess Corporation for collectors. A series of four drinking glasses are available for sale to customers at Hess service stations during the summer months.

These glasses depict color photos of toy trucks sold in previous years on the front of the glass, and a description of what the picture represents on the rear of the glass.

These glasses are a splendid addition to the series of trucks created by Hess in prior years which are so highly prized by toy collectors all over the United States.

I predict that this latest promotional item by Hess will be an instant success and I am pleased that Hess has finally recognized the collector market.

Hess Fire Truck Bank
The First Hess Truck
Hess Trailer and Racer
Hess Tanker Truck

Sources

Christmas on Wheels	(1986)
Hess Annual Report	(1970)
Hess Annual Report	(1964)
The Scope of Hess	(1964)

(All of the above are Hess Company publications.)

The New York Times	(December 15, 1993)
The Daily News	(December 10, 1993)
The Star Ledger	(December 7, 1995)
Toy Shop Magazine	(Nov/Dec 1992)
Courier News	(Date Unknown)
Forbes Magazine	(December 1995)

Acknowledgements

We would like to especially acknowledge the following people. Without their diligent work, this book would have been impossible to present. We thank:

Bill Boise
Douglas W. Campbell
Andy "Pooch" Cappuccio
Florin De Vries
Susan Doll
John P. Gulino
Jimmy Kane
Robert P. Powers
Lucille M. Russo

Epilogue

Since my last writing in the Spring of 1991, approximately fifteen major oil companies have begun marketing their logos and company trademarks on limited edition plastic promotional toy trucks or vehicles. Prior to this, only Hess, followed by Wilco and Service (known as Servco today), established a holiday premium. Although many of these other oil companies' promotionals have smartly escalated in value and collectibility, Hess is truly creator and current leader of this unique marketing program.

Another important reason why a Hess collection is so desirable and one of the hottest collectibles of the 90's is that with patience and time, an entire collection of 29 trucks is still obtainable. Over the past several years, I have helped many collectors finish and fill their personal Hess collections. Many have become my friends. It has been a rewarding experience to see the delight on their faces as they obtain each new piece.

Every year children, customers and collectors alike look forward to the newest toy vehicle from the enterprising people at Amerada Hess. Even in the middle of summer as we pass the clean white and green Hess service stations along the highways, we are already anticipating the next holiday season with high hopes and expectations.

For children, the toy makes an outstanding present. For customers, it makes a valued gift. For collectors, it's all of the above plus the love of an appreciating asset that they can proudly display on their shelves. For me personally, it's the continuation of a childhood activity that has played a special role in my life.

111

112